Addressing Domestic Violence in the Church

Helga Edwards BRE, BA, MSW

&

Bob Edwards BRE, BA, MSW

ISBN: 1977700691
ISBN-13: 978-1977700698

DEDICATION

For the sheep among the wolves, you are not
forgotten. Jesus leaves the ninety-nine to search for
the one.

CONTENTS

ACKNOWLEDGMENTS

We give all thanks to Jesus, the Good Shepherd. "He will feed His flock like a shepherd. He will carry the lambs in His arms, holding them close to His heart. He will gently lead the mother sheep with their young" (Isaiah 40:11).

Authors' Note

This book is designed to provide information in regard to the subject matter covered. It is presented with the understanding that the authors are not engaged in providing psychological, financial, legal or other professional services. If expert assistance or counseling is needed, the services of a competent professional should be sought.

1 Introduction

As therapists and Christians, we have observed that some churches do not work together with shelters to help abused women of faith. We have also seen that some abused Christian women are reluctant to meet with secular counselors for fear that the counselors will misunderstand the importance of their faith, and insist that they renounce it. These women have felt awkward with secular counselors, and some have tried to hide their religious identity. Other counselors and researchers have also found this to be a problem (Thurston 2000; Nason-Clark 2003). On the other hand, "some practitioners are concerned that religious beliefs, in some cases, facilitate violence against wives or discourage wives from seeking help when they are abused. Others worry that clergy will persuade women to return to their abusive homes (Nason-Clark, 2004). In fact, few mental health specialists are trained to understand or assess religious dynamics" (Weaver, Koenig & Larson, 1997).[1]

In this book, we hope to help bridge the gap between domestic violence services and churches, between secular counselors and abused women of faith. We wish to educate both churches and those who work with abused women about harmful misinterpretations of the Bible related to "submission," "headship," and "marital permanence." In this book we also wish to educate churches about the following topics: codependence, identifying and responding to abuse, why men abuse, and the danger of enabling abuse to continue. We hope this will be a resource to help women find freedom from abusive situations. We also hope that they will find support and understanding *both* in their churches and from domestic violence services. As Rev. Amy Gopp Director of Member Relations and Pastoral Care at Church World Service explains, there is a need to "educate faith leaders about the importance of reaching out to domestic violence programs in their communities and creating strong partnerships so that survivors are served in the way they deserve."[2]

2 Domestic Violence and the Church

The United Nations defines violence against women as, "Any act of gender based violence that results in, or is likely to result in, physical, sexual or psychological harm or suffering to women, including threats of such acts, coercion or arbitrary deprivation of liberty, whether occurring in public or in private life."[3]

It is a sad reality that domestic violence happens in church communities. One study showed that 22% of perpetrators of domestic violence and abuse go to church regularly (as cited in Baker, 2010).[4]

In 2014, the Canadian Women's Foundation[5] shared the following statistics:

- Women are twice as likely as men to be victims of family violence.[6]

- Women who experience spousal violence are more likely to endure extreme forms of assault including choking, beating, being threatened with a knife or gun, and sexual violence.[7]

- About 80% of victims of dating violence are women.[8]

- Girls are 1.5 times more likely than boys to experience violence at home.[9]

The impact of domestic violence on a woman's health is significant. In 2013, the World Health Organization highlighted that intimate partner violence was linked to the following outcomes:

- Death from homicide

- A wide range of non-fatal injuries: "The head neck and face are the most common locations of injuries, followed by musculoskeletal injuries and genital injuries."

- Symptoms of Post Traumatic Stress Disorder (Re-experiencing the trauma through intrusive thoughts, images, memories, emotions and nightmares; emotional numbness and dissociation; avoidance of places, people, and activities that are reminders of the trauma; increased arousal such as difficulty sleeping and concentrating, feeling jumpy, and being easily irritated and angered)[10]

- Depression

- Anxiety

- Suicide

- Substance Abuse

- Sexually Transmitted Disease

- Induced Abortion[11]

According to the Canadian Women's Foundation,[12] children who witness domestic violence are also significantly impacted:

- Although adults may think "the kids don't know," research shows children see or hear many domestic violence assaults.[13]

- Children who witness 10 or more incidents of parental domestic violence before the age of 16 are at least twice as likely to attempt suicide.[14]

- Children who witness violence in the home have twice the rate of psychiatric disorders as children from non-violent homes.[15]

- Domestic violence is more common in homes with young children than homes with older children.[16]

- A child who witnesses spousal violence is experiencing a form of child abuse, since research shows that "witnessing family violence is as harmful as experiencing it directly."[17]

- Exposure to violence can affect children's brain development and ability to learn, and lead to a wide range of behavioral and emotional issues such as anxiety, aggression, bullying and phobias.[18]

- Research shows that children who witness violence are more likely to grow up to become victims or abusers.[19]

An ABC News 7.30 investigation into the connection between domestic violence and religion interviewed Annette Gillespie, the CEO of Safe Steps Family Violence Centre. Annette said that in 20 years of working with victims of domestic violence, she found it was "extremely common" that women would be "encouraged by the church to stay in an abusive relationship."[20]

The same ABC News program reported that global research done in 2015 "analyzed data from 66 surveys across 44 countries, covering the expanse of almost half a million women." This study, published in the Lancet, found that the "greatest predictor of partner violence was 'environments that support male control,' especially 'norms related to male authority over female behavior.'"[21] The investigation found that "faith leaders are often uninformed, ill-equipped to respond to violence, and often don't know what kind of advice to give."[22]

According to another study, cited in Ed Stetzer's article, "The Church and its Response to Domestic and Sexual Violence," "pastors underestimate the pervasiveness of sexual and domestic violence in their congregations" (World Health Organization, 2013). Similarly, Monica Taffinder, a Christian counselor who specializes in trauma recovery, shared her observation that "many pastors tend to be somewhat naive when it comes to the probability that both victims and perpetrators exist within their church." On a positive note, Stetzer shared that 81 percent of the pastors surveyed said that they would "take appropriate action to reduce sexual and domestic violence *if they had the training and resources to do so.*"[23]

3 Patriarchy and the Bible

In his article entitled "Patriarchy and Domestic Violence: Challenging Common Misconceptions," Steven R.Tracy states, "While patriarchy may not be the overarching cause of all abuse, it is an enormously significant factor, because in traditional patriarchy males have a disproportionate share of power."[24]

The following information, taken from "The Equality Workbook: Freedom in Christ from the Oppression of Patriarchy,"[25] explains how the Christian faith became confused with patriarchy, otherwise known as "the rule of men."

The part of the Bible called the Old Testament was originally written in Hebrew. The part called the New Testament was originally written in Greek. Many Christians believe that the original Hebrew and Greek writings of the Bible were inspired by God's Holy Spirit, and are inerrant. However, imperfect human beings, including men with a bias against women, have contributed to problems with Bible *translation and commentary.*

In the 4th century AD, Christianity became the official religion of the Roman Empire. Shortly thereafter, both Old and New Testaments were translated into Rome's official language: Latin.[26]

Beginning with this translation, the meaning of passages within the Bible concerning women began to change.

Rome was a very patriarchal culture.[27] In other words, men held power in government, religion and in their households. To a large extent, a Roman worldview was also shaped by an ancient Greek philosophy called Platonism.[28] Platonism was also very patriarchal, teaching that the "inferior desires" of "women and slaves" must be "held down" by the "virtuous desires and wisdom" of free men.[29] Platonism was dualistic. In other words, all of life was divided into "superior" and "inferior" categories. The mind and the spirit were viewed as superior to the body and the emotions; men were viewed as superior to women; free men were viewed as superior to slaves. Platonism was also hierarchical. Plato believed that the superior must "rule over" the inferior in every aspect of life.[30] This hierarchy was described as the "order in nature"[31] or "natural order"[32] of things.

By the 3rd century, Platonism had become very spiritual. New Platonists (called "Neoplatonists") taught that embracing the hierarchical "order in nature" would help people move closer to God. In this so-called "natural order" men had to rule over women, and the spirit had to rule over the body *completely.*[33] The body was viewed as a prison for the soul. The connection between body and soul had to be "severed."[34] It was not enough to manage or regulate the body's impulses; they had to be *extinguished.* The translator of the Latin Bible, St.

11

Jerome, was strongly influenced by this philosophy through the commentary work of a man named Origen.[35] (A "commentary" is a book that shares the author's *interpretation* of Bible passages; it is not to be confused with the Bible itself.)

In the 3rd century AD, Origen attended a Neoplatonic academy in Alexandria.[36] The philosophy he learned there influenced him to view God and the Bible in hierarchical terms. He began to view the Trinity as an eternal hierarchy of persons, in which the *inferior* Son and Spirit were seen as subordinate to the all-powerful Father.[37] He also applied this hierarchical perspective to relationships between men and women. Another student of this academy was a non-Christian philosopher named Plotinus.[38] Plotinus' books, called *the Enneads*, strongly influenced the 4th century AD commentary work of St. Augustine, the Bishop of Hippo.[39] In his Confessions, Augustine praises "the books of the Platonists," and explains that they helped him to make sense of the Bible.[40] Augustine "accepted a patriarchal system that justified [domestic violence] and made battered women ultimately responsible for being beaten, by not being submissive enough to their husbands."[41]

St. Jerome's Latin translation of the Bible and St. Augustine's commentaries removed Bible passages from their original languages and contexts, and placed them into a very hierarchical Neoplatonic framework. These developments significantly influenced the emergence of patriarchal theology in the church.

A careful study of the lives of some of the most influential theologians of the 3rd and 4th centuries AD reveals that those largely responsible for a patriarchal shift in Bible translation and commentary (Origen, Jerome, Augustine, Chrysostom) were all strongly influenced by Neoplatonic philosophy. This is a very important observation. Neoplatonism along with the patriarchal norms of Roman society influenced these men to translate and interpret the Bible with a *systematic bias against women.* Even when Bible passages would say nothing about women being subordinate to men, these theologians would *infer* male authority from the text. (An inference is not something stated by the author of a text; it is something that is assumed by the reader).

In the 16th century AD, this bias against women was carried over into the Protestant Reformation by theologians such as John Calvin, who relied heavily on the commentaries of St. Augustine to develop his own views.[42] St. Jerome's bias in Bible translation was also carried over into a 16th century Latin version of the Bible, written by a man named Erasmus--*yet another Neoplatonist.*[43] Erasmus' Latin translation became the basis of the first English translations of the Bible, which still influence how the Bible is understood today.[44]

Some in the church have suggested that if we question the translation or interpretation of Bible verses concerning women, then we are "undermining the authority of God's Word," and calling every principle it teaches into question. This is simply not accurate. Neoplatonism influenced some theologians and translators in very systematic and identifiable ways. Though this error is pervasive, it does not affect what the Bible has to say about other important issues. Confidence in the Bible's message is likely to increase once the bias of patriarchal culture and philosophy is removed. Credibility is enhanced when errors in translation are recognized and corrected, rather than denied.

4 "Submission"

Neoplatonists such as Origen, Augustine, Jerome and Chrysostom first changed the meaning of the creation story in Genesis by forcing it to fit into a hierarchical, male-dominated worldview (for further information see chapter 2 of "The Equality Workbook: Freedom in Christ from the Oppression of Patriarhcy").[45] This error then served to alter their understanding of the apostle Paul's letters, since Paul often makes reference to the creation account. These two errors together led patriarchal theologians to the erroneous conclusion that God intended men to rule over women in the church. It also led them to the conclusion that it is God's will for men to rule over women in Christian homes.

Paul's Letter to the Ephesians

Paul's alleged command in Ephesians 5:22, "Wives *submit* to your husbands," forms the foundation of the complementarian view that husbands must exercise authority over their wives in Christian marriage.[46] ("Complementarian" is a contemporary term or euphemism for "patriarchal.") This supposed command to wives is often supplemented and reinforced by headings that have been added to the biblical text by translators. Immediately above Ephesians 5:22 in the Open Bible: New King James

Version, for example, we read the heading, "Wives: Submit to Your Husbands." The New American Standard Version *adds* yet another imperative statement directed exclusively to wives in Ephesians 5:24: "But as the church is subject to Christ, so also the wives *ought to be* to their husbands in everything."

In the oldest available Greek manuscripts of the New Testament (Parchment 46 and Codex Vaticanus), Ephesians 5:22 does *not* say, "Wives *submit* to your husbands."[47] Neither the heading, "Wives Submit to Your Husbands," nor the additional phrase in Ephesians 5:24 telling wives that they "ought to be" submissive can be found in *any* Greek manuscripts whatsoever.

In this passage, the apostle Paul introduces the idea of "submission" in Ephesians 5:21. After telling *all Christians* to "be filled with the Spirit" in Ephesians 5:18, he then explains what this will look like: "submitting one to another out of reverence for Christ" (Ephesians 5:21). In other words, *all* Christians who are filled with the Holy Spirit are *to voluntarily assume a disposition of love and humility towards one another*. Ephesians 5:22 then adds the phrase "wives to your husbands" as an *example* of what this mutual submission will look like.

In grammatical terms *"be filled* with the Spirit" is the imperative verb; "submitting one to another" is a participle phrase (that describes being filled with the Spirit); and "wives to your husbands" is yet another phrase that qualifies "submitting one to another" by

16

providing an example. Simply put, "wives to your husbands" is *not* a complete sentence; it *cannot* stand on its own as a separate command. *There is no new and separate command directed only to wives.* Patriarchal translators create the *illusion* that there are two different kinds of commands--one in Ephesians 5:21 directed to all Christians, and another in Ephesians 5:22 directed exclusively to wives. The *added* command *appears* to reinforce a gender-based hierarchy in Christian homes. It is important to recognize that this is not grammatically possible in the Greek text of the oldest available manuscripts. It is only possible if a second imperative verb is *inserted* into verse 22.[48] The submission that exists in marriage from wives to husbands is *one example* of the humility and loving service that *all Christians who are filled with the Spirit* are called upon to demonstrate.

In Ephesians 5:24 Paul does not tell wives that they "ought to be" submissive to their husbands. Rather, he makes an *observation* regarding "the way things were" in ancient Greek, Roman and Jewish cultures. The verb he uses in verse 24 in reference to wives is *"hupotassetai"* (*are subject*); it is a *present, indicative, middle or passive* verb. When understood in the *passive* voice, it is *not* a command; rather, it is used to *describe* something *as it already is*.[49] The same verb, in the same tense, mood and voice is used in Luke 10:20: "Nevertheless do not rejoice in this, that the spirits *are subject* (*hupotassetai*) to you, but rejoice that your names are recorded in heaven" (NASB). The disciples discovered that demonic spirits "were subject" to them, in Jesus' name. This was not a command; it was an observation. The same verb, in the same tense, mood and voice is used again in 1 Corinthians 14:32: "and the spirits of prophets are subject (*hupotassetai*) to prophets" (NASB). Paul is explaining that a prophet's spirit "is subject" to him or her. This means that people have control over when and how they might prophesy. Again, this is an observation, not a command.

When the biblical authors talk about what someone "should" or "ought" to do, they typically make use of the Greek words "*opheilo*" or "*dei.*"[50] One example of such a statement is found in Luke 13:14: "But the synagogue official, indignant because Jesus had healed on the Sabbath, began saying to the crowd in response, 'There are six days in which work should (*dei*) be done; so come during them and get healed, and not on the Sabbath day.'" The teachers of the Law are telling people how they "should" behave. They are talking about an obligation, expectation or command. They are telling people what to do. Another example is found in Luke 18:1: "Now He was telling them a parable to show that at all times they ought (*dein*) to pray and not to lose heart" (NASB). Jesus was telling his disciples what they "ought to" do. He is giving them instructions that they are meant to follow.

Paul's use of *hupotassetai* (*are subject*) with regard to wives in Ephesians 5:24 is the same as Luke's use of *the same word* regarding demonic spirits *and* the spirits of the prophets. In these texts, the Greek words *opheilo* and *dei* are absent. Translators of the NASB version of the Bible acknowledge that they have *added* the phrase "ought to be" to the text of Ephesians 5:24.[51] This phrase is not found in *any* Greek manuscripts of this passage.[52] *Paul is not telling wives what they "ought to" do; rather he is describing a situation that already existed at the time he wrote his letter.*

To understand the situation Paul is referring to, it is helpful to become familiar with the Greco-Roman and Jewish literature of the New Testament era, concerning the relationship between husbands and wives. According to Greek philosophy, which was embraced throughout the Roman Empire, a man was indeed in charge of his household, and women were "subject" to his authority. According to Aristotle, women were to be viewed as the slaves and possessions of a man.[53] A similar view of women was proposed by the Jewish philosopher, Philo of Alexandria.[54] In the eyes of 1st century Greeks, Romans and Jews, men did indeed exercise authority over women, children and slaves.

This is the culture Paul is addressing in his letter, and he correctly observes that wives "are subject" to husbands. *Instead of affirming this role, however, Paul says something very different*; he tells husbands to imitate the love of Jesus, who laid aside His divine authority to make Himself a servant: "Husbands, love your wives, just as Christ loved the church and gave Himself up for her" (Ephesians 5:25). Unlike the passive verb Paul uses to describe the pre-existing submission of wives, the verb directed towards husbands is *present, active and imperative*. Simply put, it *is* a command. Paul is indeed telling husbands what they "ought to" do. In fact, he uses this exact language not with wives, but rather with husbands in Ephesians 5:28: "So ought [*ophelousin*] husbands to love their wives." This is not a command that Greek, Roman or Jewish men would have been accustomed to hearing. Men filled with the Spirit, however, would "submit" themselves to other Christians-- including women, including their wives: "submit one to another out of reverence for Christ."

In its original language and cultural context, how might we understand the apostle Paul's overall message in Ephesians 5:18-28? **Everyone, be filled with the Spirit, submitting one to another, just as wives do to husbands, and just as the church does to Christ. Husbands, you ought also to love and serve your wives, just as Christ loved and served the church, giving His life for her on the cross.**

A patriarchal/complementarian reading of Ephesians 5:21-28 rejects the notion of mutual submission in Christian marriage. It insists that just as Jesus was the "leader" of the church, so too must a husband be the "leader" of his wife. In other words, according to patriarchal theology, it is the "leadership" of Jesus that husbands are told to imitate in marriage.

Jesus fills many roles in His relationship to the church. He is our Leader. He is our High Priest. He is the Good Shepherd. He is our Teacher. He is the Chief Cornerstone of God's living temple, the church. He made Himself a servant and died on the cross to atone for our sins. ("Sin" is when people choose to do what they know is wrong.) Among all of these aspects of Christ's ministry on earth, husbands are told to imitate *only one*: *"Husbands, love your wives, just as Christ loved the church and gave Himself up for her"* (Ephesians 5:25). Husbands, love your wives, make yourselves a servant, just as Christ loved and served the church. ("Church" in a New Testament context is not a religious institution. Rather, it is the community of all people who trust and follow Jesus Christ as their God, Forgiver and Friend.)

The apostle Paul teaches the same principle of *mutual* servanthood in his letter to the Philippians. All of Christ's followers are to have the same "mindset" of love and humility towards one another:

> In your relationships with one another, have the same mindset as Christ Jesus: Who, being in very nature God, did not consider equality with God something to be used to His own advantage; rather, He made himself nothing by taking the very nature of a servant, being made in human likeness. And being found in appearance as a man, He humbled himself by becoming obedient to death--even death on a cross! (Philippians 2:5-8)

Jesus reminds His followers that they have *One Leader*, and that is Christ alone. *All* of Jesus' followers are "siblings" and "equals":

> *Do not be called leaders*; for One is your Leader, that is, Christ. But the greatest among you shall be your servant. Whoever exalts

himself shall be humbled; and whoever
humbles himself shall be exalted. (Matthew
23:10-12, NASB)

Every Christian is called to love as Christ has loved
us (John 13:34-35). In Christian homes, *husbands
are called to love, **not** to be the leaders of their wives.*

Paul's Letter to the Colossians

Paul's message to husbands in the church of Ephesus
is repeated in his letter to the Colossians: "Husbands,
love your wives and do not be harsh with them"
(Colossians 3:19, NIV). Once again, Paul's choice of
Greek words here is significant. Husbands are to
"love" (*agapate)* with a Christ-like, unconditional
love, that lays down its life for others. Jesus uses the
same language of *His own love* for the church in the
following passage: "Greater love (*agapen*) has no one
than this: to lay down one's life for one's friends"
(John 15:13, NIV). Paul contrasts *this kind of love*
with "harshness" (*pikrainesthe*); which can also be
understood as "bitterness" or "cruelty." The root of
the word chosen by Paul is *pikros,* which Aristotle
used to describe the rule of an "embittered tyrant" in
his "Athenian Constitutions" (chapter 19). In sharp
contrast to the "rulers of the Gentiles," husbands are
commanded to love like Christ, who came to earth not
to be served, but rather to serve (c.f. Matthew 20:25-
28). Jesus provides a picture of this love and service
when He dresses Himself like a slave, washes the
disciples feet, and then tells them to imitate what He
has done: "For I have set you an example, that you

also should do as I have done to you" (John 13:15, NRSV).

In Colossians 3:18 and 20, Paul also provides instructions for wives and children. Unlike Paul's instructions to children, wives are *not* told to "obey" (*hupakouete*) their husbands. Rather, Paul uses the same language that can be found in Ephesians 5:21; he encourages wives to exemplify the same kind of mutual submission (*hupotassesthe) that is required of all Christians.*

Though patriarchal theology *infers* from Paul's letters to Ephesus and Colossae that men should rule over women in Christian marriage, the apostle Paul's original language, understood in its original context, paints a picture of mutual love, humility and service.

Peter's First Letter

If patriarchal men cannot use Paul's letters to Ephesus and Colossae to justify their control of women, they will sometimes turn to 1st Peter. Rationalizing male authority and female submission, however, requires that Peter's comments be viewed very selectively, *and* taken out of context.

Chapters 2 and 3 of Peter's first letter encourage followers of Jesus to demonstrate Christ's love and humility, even in situations that are unfair: "When they hurled their insults at Him, He did not retaliate; when He suffered, He made no threats. Instead, He entrusted Himself to Him who judges justly" (1 Peter 2:23). The focus of these chapters is on **not**

returning evil for evil in situations that are unjust. The apostle Paul shares a similar message in his letter to the Romans:

> Do not repay anyone evil for evil... If it is possible, as far as it depends on you, live at peace with everyone. Do not take revenge, my dear friends, but leave room for God's wrath, for it is written: "It is mine to avenge; I will repay," says the Lord... Do not be overcome by evil, but overcome evil with good. (Romans 12:17-21)

1st Peter chapter 2 does not condone slavery, but simply recognizes its existence in the 1st century Roman Empire. Even with masters that are unfair "skoliois"[55] (literally bent, crooked), slaves are to imitate Christ's love. It is important to remember, however, that Paul encourages slaves to *gain their freedom if it is at all possible to do so* (1 Corinthians 7:21).

Wives likewise are to demonstrate Christ's love in their marriages, even with husbands that are unbelievers. Peter uses the same word in his instructions to wives, "submit," as Paul uses in his instructions to *all* Christians in Ephesians 5:21: "Submit one to another out of reverence for Christ." In both passages, the verb "submit" is in the *middle voice*, which means it is a *reflexive action performed by the self, upon the self.* "The middle voice in Greek has no exact parallel in the English language,"[56] so it can be difficult for people to understand this word.

"Submit" here means to *voluntarily assume a disposition of love and humility towards others.* It is not about a sense of duty or obligation to others.

Husbands who *are* believers are reminded to "likewise" imitate Christ, and be considerate towards their wives. They are reminded that their wives are co-heirs with them in God's kingdom. God tells husbands that if they do not treat their wives with honor, He will not hear their prayers (1 Peter 3:7). Abraham, Sarah's husband, is addressed as "lord" in this chapter, but it is important to remember that this term in its original context was *simply a term of respect used even to address servants* (see Genesis 24:17-18).

In 1 Peter 3:4, some English translations say that women are to be "gentle" and "quiet." Some infer that this means women are to be "subservient," the opposite of "having authority." In the Greek language, however, the first word, "praeos," is the opposite of "agriotes": *"savageness, fierceness, cruelty."*[57] Similarly, the second word "hesuchiou" properly refers to being "calm"--"the opposite of *violence*, not the opposite of authority or power" (Wilshire, 2010, p. 29). Both of these terms represent the opposite of being *vengeful,* in keeping with the overall message of Peter's letter.

The New Living Translation of the Bible injects a strong patriarchal bias into Peter's letter by twice telling wives to "accept the authority" of their husbands (1 Peter 3:1 and 5). In the original Greek language of this passage there is **absolutely no reference to a husband's alleged "authority."** As stated, Peter uses the same language here as Paul in Ephesians. He tells wives to "hupotassomenai" (adopt a disposition of love and humility towards their husbands)--the same form of "submission" *all Christians* (male and female) are to have towards one another.

English translations tell us that Sarah "obeyed" Abraham in 1 Peter 3:6. It has been suggested that this language tells us that Sarah was acknowledging Abraham's "male authority" over her. Once again, however, the Greek language of the passage does not suggest this. The word used to describe Sarah's response to Abraham is "hupekousen"; though this can mean "obey" in certain contexts, the same word was also used to describe the actions of judges (authority figures) who would "give a hearing" to people in court:

> Cyrus, however, would not be at leisure for a long time to **give such men a hearing (hupakouein),** and when he did **give them a hearing (akouseien)** he would postpone the trial for a long time. By so doing he thought he would accustom them to pay their court and that he would thus excite less ill-feeling than he would if he compelled them to come by imposing penalties.[58]

The two Greek verbs used to describe a judge **"giving a hearing"** to those summoned to court are

"hupakouein" and **"akouseien."** These words are used *interchangeably*. They were often used in ancient Greek literature to refer to "paying heed, listening, or giving a hearing to someone."[59]

It is important to note that while **"hupakouein" is used of Sarah** in 1st Peter 3:6, **"akouseien" is used of Abraham** in the Greek Septuagint version of the following passage: "Listen (akoue) to whatever Sarah tells you, because it is through Isaac that your offspring will be reckoned" (Genesis 21:12).[60] In other words, both Sarah and Abraham "paid heed" to one another in their marriage relationship. The original language of 1st Peter does not suggest a male-dominated social hierarchy in marriage. This notion has been wrongly inferred by patriarchal theologians.

After discussing slaves, wives and husbands, Peter reminds all Christians to be humble and loving, imitating Christ, no matter what situation they find themselves in--the overall theme of this entire section of 1st Peter.

1st Peter is not meant to represent a male-dominated hierarchy in the home as "God's will," anymore than it is meant to condone the injustice of slavery. As Carolyn Custis James states, **patriarchy is the backdrop of the Bible, not the message.**[61] In Christ, "there is neither Jew nor Gentile, neither slave nor free, nor is there male and female, for you are all one in Christ Jesus" (Galatians 3:28). Throughout history, whenever this verse has been genuinely applied, it has brought transformation and freedom to human hearts and relationships.

When Paul and Peter write to the churches about how husbands and wives should relate to one another "in Christ," they acknowledge the patriarchal norms of the day, *without endorsing them*. They then do the unthinkable, and tell husbands to love and honor their wives in the same way they themselves are to be loved and honored; husbands and wives are to "submit one to another out of reverence for Christ" (Ephesians 5:21).

Here we see the wisdom of God. In the New Testament, God spoke to the situations of the day. He advised wives and slaves to "be submissive" (to voluntarily assume a disposition of love and humility) even towards people who were unfair. Then He addressed those who held power, telling them *to lay that power down*. Husbands were to "likewise" love and serve their wives (1 Peter 3:7). Masters were to regard slaves as family (Philemon 16-17), showing love and humility towards them "in the same manner" (Ephesians 6:9). If both parties lived like this, then injustice, abuse and even these social hierarchies would come to an end.

Writing to churches that were being told they must obey oppressive religious traditions, the apostle Paul made the following comments:

> You were bought with a price; do not become slaves of men (1 Corinthians 7:23).

> It is for freedom that Christ has set us free.
> Stand firm, then, and do not let yourselves be
> burdened again by a yoke of slavery
> (Galatians 5:1).

One of these oppressive traditions was the practice of male authority. (For more information, see chapter 5 of "The Equality Workbook: Freedom in Christ from the Oppression of Patriarchy.")

The Bible does *not* say that a male-dominated hierarchy is God's will. It does *not* tell people to stay in abusive relationships. It *does* say not to seek revenge. It *does* say, "Learn to do right; seek justice. Defend the oppressed" (Isaiah 1:17). Christians can seek justice with a heart of love and humility, instead of an attitude of vengeance. Believers can have this disposition while taking care of themselves, and standing up against injustice. Christians can be loving and not vengeful while seeking safety, having protective boundaries, and not allowing injustice to continue.

Having a disposition of love and humility does *not* mean people are to annihilate their emotions. Victims of domestic violence naturally experience feelings of grief, sadness, anger, stress and pain. Jesus Himself was a "man of sorrows, acquainted with grief" (Isaiah 53:3). Psalm 4:4 says, "Be angry and do not sin." We can *feel* angry, but we are not to hurt ourselves or others with our anger. Jesus was angry at the Pharisees, the religious leaders of the day, for oppressing the people (Mark 3:1-5). Anger can energize people to cope actively, to seek justice and to defend the oppressed. If people do not acknowledge their anger and do not express it *in healthy ways*, they may end up struggling with ulcers, muscle tension, headaches or anxiety. Sometimes depression can be caused by buried or denied anger.

"Turning the Other Cheek"

When Jesus told His followers to "turn the other cheek" (Matthew 5:39), this was also *about not taking personal revenge.* As with other Bible passages, the original language and context of Jesus' words can help us better understand their meaning. In Matthew's gospel, Jesus advises His followers not to "antistenai" someone who has done them wrong. In ancient Greek literature, "antistenai" was used to mean "resisting" someone by "matching" their behavior.[62] The context of Jesus' instructions affirms this meaning: "You have heard that it was said, 'An eye for an eye and a tooth for a tooth.' But I say to you, do not resist (antistenai) the evildoer. But whoever strikes you on the right cheek, turn the other to him as well" (Matthew 5:38-39). If someone strikes you on the cheek, you are not to respond by vengefully striking them back in the same manner. Turning the other cheek means *not returning evil for evil*. We are to show our enemies love, not to return hatred for hatred (Matthew 5:43-44). It refers to personal retaliation, not to seeking justice in the case of a criminal offence, or to defending oneself in the case of aggression. "Turning the other cheek" does *not* mean we cannot stand up for justice, and it does *not* exclude going to the authorities.

"Lawsuits" Among Believers

Some claim that the Bible instructs Christians not to take other believers to court. In light of this, women in abusive relationships may be discouraged from contacting the authorities. In 1 Corinthians 6:1-8 Paul rebukes Christians for "cheating" one another, and going to civil court for rulings on "trivial cases" regarding material "disputes." Paul wishes these Christians would stop cheating one another and would at least seek another believer to arbitrate between them, rather than bringing these "smallest matters" to the secular courts. He rebukes the church for not modeling Christ-like virtues to their neighbors. Paul also reminds the Corinthians that "thieves, coveters and swindlers" will not "inherit the kingdom of God" (1 Corinthians 6:10). This is *not* a prohibition against contacting the authorities when a *crime* has been committed. In the book of Romans Paul says, "For the one in authority is God's servant for your good. But if you do wrong, be afraid, for rulers do not bear the sword for no reason. They are God's servants, agents of wrath to bring punishment on the wrongdoer" (Romans 13:4). *Christians are free to contact the authorities and bring the situation to court when a crime has been committed against them.*

5 "Headship"

The notion that men are meant to "have authority" over wives in their homes is also based on a fundamental misunderstanding of "head/body" metaphors found in the New Testament.

The word "head" can have many different meanings, depending upon its context. In today's corporate world, for example, the "head" of a company is often the Chief Executive Officer (CEO): the person "in charge." On naval vessels, however, the word "head" refers to a ship's toilet. The same word, in the same language, can have vastly different meanings, depending on its context.

In the Greek language of the New Testament, the word translated "head" in reference to husbands is "kephale." In ancient Greek literature, this word was commonly used to refer to the "source" of something. In the context of husbands and wives in the New Testament, kephale *always* carries this meaning. The Greek word more often used to mean "ruler" was "*archon.*"[63] In Greek literature outside of the Bible, *kephale* was used in reference to the Greek god Zeus, as the *source* or origin of all things: "Zeus is the *head (kephale)*, Zeus the centre, from Zeus comes all that is."[64] Head (kephale) was also used to describe the "source" of a river: "From the *headwaters (kephalai)* of the river Tearus flows the best and finest water of all."[65]

The apostle Paul uses kephale in this sense in his letter to the Ephesians to explain that Jesus Christ is the source of Christian growth and maturity:

> Instead, speaking the truth in love, we will grow to become in every respect the mature body of Him who is the *head (kephale)*, that is, Christ. *From Him the whole body*, joined and held together by every supporting ligament, *grows* and builds itself up in love, as each part does its work. (Ephesians 4:15-16)

Paul uses the same language with the same meaning in his letter to the Colossian church:

> They have lost connection with the *head (kephale), from whom the whole body*, supported and held together by its ligaments and sinews, *grows* as God causes it to grow. (Colossians 2:19)

The same word, *kephale* (head), is used in 1st Corinthians to refer to the first man, Adam, as the "source" of the first woman, Eve:

> But I want you to realize that the head of every man is Christ, and the *head (kephale)* of the woman is man, and the head of Christ is God. (1 Corinthians 11:3)

The human race was created through Christ (John 1:3); He is the "source" of "every man." Adam, the first man, was the "source" of Eve, the first woman, since she was taken from his side (Genesis 2:22). God was the miraculous source of Jesus' incarnation as a human being (Luke 1:35).

Some complementarians insist that 1 Corinthians 11:3 speaks of God as the "authority over" Christ, Christ as the "authority over" man, and man as the "authority over" woman. The context of the passage, however, does *not* support this meaning. In 1 Corinthians 11:11-12, Paul reminds the Corinthian church that just as a man was the source of the first woman, so too is a woman the source of every man: "For although the first woman came from man, every other man was born from a woman, and everything comes from God" (1 Cor. 11:12). Paul *is* talking about *source* in the immediate context of this passage, *not authority*.

Despite all of these New Testament uses of "kephale" to mean "source," some complementarians will insist that "head" means "authority." Sometimes they will cite the following passages:

> And He is the head (kephale) of the body, the church; He is the **beginning** and the firstborn from among the dead, so that in everything He might have the supremacy. (Colossians 1:18)

and

> …having raised Him out from the dead, and having set Him at His right hand in the heavenly realms, above every principality and

authority and power and dominion, and every name being named, not only in this age, but also in the one coming. And He put all things under His feet and gave Him to be head (kephale) over all things to the church, which is His body, the fullness of the One filling all in all. (Ephesians 1:20-23)

In English translations of the Bible, it may appear that these passages use "head" in reference to Christ's authority over the church. However, looking carefully at the Greek language and context of these passages, it is evident that Paul is referring to Christ as the **source** of the church's authority over demonic principalities and powers.

Following His resurrection from the dead and His ascension into heaven, Jesus Christ is presented as having authority over *demonic principalities and powers*: "For we wrestle not against flesh and blood, but against *principalities*, against *powers*, against the *rulers of the darkness* of this world, against *spiritual wickedness* in high places" (Ephesians 6:12).

Jesus is now seated far above these principalities and powers, and we--His body, which is connected to the head--are seated there with Him: "And God raised us up with Christ and seated us with Him in the heavenly realms in Christ Jesus" (Ephesians 2:6).

Jesus has authority over these demonic powers, *and so does the church*, in our union with Christ. How did Jesus set the church free from the power of demonic oppression? By taking upon Himself the form of a servant and dying on the cross: "And having disarmed the powers and authorities, He made a public spectacle of them, triumphing over them by the cross" (Colossians 2:15).

Through His death and resurrection, He became the "firstborn from among the dead." In other words, when Jesus died and rose again, He became the *source* of eternal life *and* authority over demonic powers to those who trust and follow Him.

When using the word "head," the point is that Jesus is the *source* of the church, our new life, our salvation, our spiritual growth, *and* our authority over demonic principalities and powers.

Jesus Himself illustrated what it means to be the "head" (the source of new life and salvation) for His followers when He shared the following parable: "Very truly I tell you, unless a kernel of wheat falls to the ground and dies, it remains only a single seed. But if it dies, it produces many seeds" (John 12:24). When Jesus died on the cross, He became the kernel of wheat that *led to the growth* of many new seeds-- all those who trust and follow Him will have eternal life.

What does "kephale" (head) mean in the New Testament? Regarding Jesus and Adam, it means "source." Adam was the "source" of Eve, who was taken from his side; and Jesus is the "source" of life, growth and freedom in the church. Referring to husbands as the "source" of their wives (Ephesians 5:23), Paul tells them, "love your wives, just as Christ loved the church and gave Himself up for her" (Ephesians 5:25). Paul's point in his letter to the Ephesians is that without Jesus taking upon Himself the form of a servant and loving us to the point of death, *there would be no church* (Jesus is the source of the church). Then he says, husbands, *you need to learn to love like this*, so that this love can be a *source* of life in your marriage. If you neglect your body, you will die. So too if you neglect to love and serve your wife, your marriage will whither.

Is this language teaching male authority? On the contrary, let's look at the example set for us by Jesus Himself:

> Jesus called them together and said, "You know that the **rulers of the Gentiles** lord it over them, and their high officials **exercise authority** over them. **Not so with you.** Instead, whoever wants to become great among you must be your servant, and whoever wants to be first must be your slave--just as the Son of Man did not come to be served, but to serve, and to give His life as a ransom for many." (Matthew 20:25-28)

Two of Jesus' disciples had just asked if they could *rule* by His side in His coming kingdom. They thought that "ruling over" others would make them "great." Jesus explained to them that "exercising authority" over others does not make a person great.

In God's kingdom, if you want to be great, you must become a servant (Matthew 23:11).

This example of **NOT** exercising authority over others is what husbands are *commanded* to imitate in the New Testament: "Husbands, love your wives, just as Christ loved the church and gave Himself up for her" (Ephesians 5:25). Suggesting that this passage means that husbands should "rule over" their wives is the *exact opposite* of what Jesus taught and modeled for us through His sacrificial love.

When Jesus took upon Himself the form of a servant, He became the "source" of our life and freedom. If a husband wants his wife to relate to him with a heart of love and humility, Paul tells him to first relate to her in this way, following the example of Christ. This is the meaning of head/body metaphors in the New Testament, as they relate to Christian marriage.

6 Codependence

If we believe we are responsible to "fix" other people and their problems, a specific destructive pattern can easily begin. Stephen B. Karpman identified this pattern, and it is known as the "The Karpman Drama Triangle."[66] It is also sometimes referred to as the "rescue triangle."

The three corners of this triangle are labeled "Rescuer," "Persecutor" and "Victim." In this pattern, we often rescue people *from their responsibilities*, and then we move to the "persecutor corner"--we feel angry at the people we try to help when we give beyond our capacity. We then move to the "victim corner" because we feel used and unappreciated. We rescue people when we believe they are unable to take responsibility for their own feelings or problems; these people are often in the "victim corner" of the triangle. After we try to "fix" their problems, victims may become angry with us (moving to the "persecutor corner") when their problems are not resolved, or if they feel we are treating them as incapable. And so, the dance around the triangle continues, and it only becomes worse over time.[67]

Mistaken teachings about "headship" push people into the "rescue triangle." Men are encouraged to be "leaders," and are told to *take responsibility* for their wives' spiritual growth. Taking responsibility for another adult's spiritual development often leads to controlling behavior. Women who do not wish to be controlled are then wrongly accused of rebelling against "godly leadership." Patriarchal men, sometimes without knowing, set themselves up as idols (false gods) in women's lives, interfering with the work of the Holy Spirit. It is not surprising that many men in the rescuer role eventually burn out, and then switch from being over-responsible to becoming under-responsible.

Many men have even assumed the role of mediator between women and God. They portray "male authority" as a protective "covering" for women. The doctrine of male authority as a "spiritual covering" for half the human race stands in direct contradiction to the apostle Paul's words concerning Jesus' role as the *exclusive* mediator between God and all humanity: "For there is one God and *one mediator* between God and humanity, Christ Jesus, Himself human" (1 Timothy 2:5). (For further information about the false doctrine of "spiritual covering," see The Equality Workbook: Freedom in Christ from the Oppression of Patriarchy, chapter 5).[68]

Rescuing is going beyond what God calls us to do when He says we are to love one another. The rescue triangle involves manipulation and control. We try to control others by "taking care" of them, or by using anger, guilt or pity to "make" others take care of us.

Sometimes patriarchy pressures women into the role of "family rescuer," having them take responsibility for the needs and feelings of their husbands and children, regardless of their age or capacity.

Codependent Sex

Codependence also gives women the message that they are responsible to "take care of" a man's sexual feelings. As a result, women often feel pressured to "submit" to unwanted sexual demands. This is what people in the "victim" and "persecutor" roles expect from "rescuers" in the Karpman Drama Triangle-- they believe the "rescuer" must take care of their feelings and/or problems *for* them. Men who treat their wives this way are violating God's overall commandments for human relationships: "Love your neighbor *as* yourself" (Mark 12:31) and "Submit *one to another out of reverence for Christ*" (Ephesians 5:21).

One Bible verse that is **mistranslated** *and* **misused** to put pressure on wives to "submit" to the sexual demands of their husbands is found in 1 Corinthians 7:4. In the English Standard Version of the Bible, the first part of this verse reads as follows: "For the wife does not have authority over her own body, but the husband does."

To begin, men who use this verse to pressure their wives for sex often stop short of reading the next sentence: "Likewise the husband does not have authority over his own body, but the wife does" (1 Corinthians 7:4). Whatever the apostle Paul is writing about in both parts of this verse is *mutual*. He is *not* talking about something women are exclusively *commanded* to do.

He *is* talking about something that *both* husbands and wives are *permitted* to do in the context of marriage. They are *allowed* to enjoy sexual union with one another, as a consummation of their marriage vows.

The word translated "have authority over" in this passage is "exousiasei." In ancient Greek literature, this word was frequently used to indicate that a person had "license" or "permission" to "indulge" in some activity:

- Philip of Macedon *"indulged"* (exousias) in a feast.[69]

- Athens was renowned for permitting *"freedom"* (exousia) of speech.[70]

- Uncivilized lands granted men *"license"* (exousias) to indulge their passions under any circumstances.[71]

- A fertility god named Apis had "a greater abundance of such *indulgences* (exousiazei) [i.e. 'the pleasure of food and sex'] than many monarchs."[72]

- An account that seems to diverge from known facts is attributed to "poetic license" (exousian).[73]

In these examples, from the 4th century BC, through the New Testament period to the 2nd century AD, ancient Greek writers used some form of exousiazei in reference to "freedom" or "license" to "indulge." Aristotle's example of the fertility god's "indulgences" uses *the exact same word as Paul, in the same tense, mood and voice.*

In 1st Corinthians 7, Paul is addressing those in the church who were teaching *an ascetic philosophy.* They considered sexual union, even within marriage, to be sinful. They taught complete abstinence from sexual intimacy, to the point of encouraging Christians to dissolve their marriages.[74] Paul quotes one of their principles in 1 Corinthians 7:1: "It is good for a man not to touch a woman," *and then proceeds to correct it.* He explains that husbands and wives should remain married, and that they "have permission" to enjoy sexual intimacy with one another. They do not "have license" to indulge themselves however they wish; but they do "have license" to enjoy sex within marriage. If a couple wished to abstain from sexual relations for the purpose of prayer, Paul advised that they do this on a temporary basis, by mutual consent. Neither the husband nor the wife is granted "authority" to demand sex from his or her spouse.

Though the word "exousia" did refer to authority *in some contexts*, **when used in the context of expressing one's passions**, it frequently meant having "license" or "permission" to engage in a certain activity--in this case, sexual union within marriage. Paul's instructions in 1st Corinthians 7:4 could be paraphrased in the following manner:

**A wife does *not* have license to do whatever she
wants sexually--she may not engage in sexual
immorality. Similarly, a husband does *not* have
license to do whatever he wants sexually--he may
not engage in sexual immorality. Both the wife
and the husband, however, *do* have license to
enjoy sexual union with one another, within the
context of their marriage.**

In a Christian marriage there should be no sexual
demands. *Each* person is to voluntarily assume a
disposition of love and humility towards the other.
Each person can state what they would like sexually,
and what they are comfortable and uncomfortable
with. The couple can then come up with ways to
share intimacy that they are *both* comfortable with. A
husband who loves his wife as he loves himself will
not pressure her for sex, or expect her to engage in
any behavior that makes her feel uncomfortable.

Unfortunately, women in abusive relationships often
experience the *opposite* of Christ-like love. For
example, in the 7.30 News investigation on the
connection between domestic violence and the
church, "Almost every single woman who had
experienced abuse in her marriage told ABC News
that her husband had raped her."[75] Barb Kiffe from
Dakota County Sexual Assault Services explains,
"Sexism is at the heart of marital rape, just as it is at
the heart of most forms of sexual violence."[76]
Abusive men use sexual violence "to maintain power
and control" over their partners.[77]

44

Marital rape has a very harmful effect on a woman's well-being. Women often experience feelings of betrayal, fear, revulsion, depression and/or anger. Women feel confusion and grief, experiencing extreme loss related to self-esteem, safety, control, broken trust, etc. Healing can be a very long and difficult process, and women can feel trapped living with their abuser, especially if the assailant is also the economic provider of the family, or the father of her children.[78]

Jesus longs to bring healing and liberation to those who are abused. Psalm 34:18 says, "God is close to the broken-hearted, and to those who are crushed in spirit." Isaiah 42:3 says, "He will not break a bruised reed or put out a flickering candle. He will bring justice to all who have been wronged." Jesus said, "The Spirit of the Lord is upon Me... He has sent Me to heal the broken-hearted, to set the captives free... to set free those who are oppressed" (Luke 4:18, Isaiah 61:1). The heart of Jesus is for the abused; He has come "to comfort all that mourn," and His "day of vengeance" is coming against those who oppress others (Isaiah 61:2).

Codependent patterns of thinking are also connected to an unhealthy emphasis on how women dress. A patriarchal worldview dictates that in order for a man to avoid sexual sin, he must exercise control over how women clothe themselves. This leads to "victim-blaming" in the case of sexual crimes perpetrated by men against women. Making women responsible for a man's sexual behavior also disempowers the man. He is made to feel that he cannot say "no" to his impulses. The Bible repeatedly states that *we are each responsible for our own choices and behaviors.* 1 Corinthians 10:13 says, "No temptation has overtaken you except what is common to humanity. And God is faithful; He will not let you be tempted beyond what you can bear. But when you are tempted, He will also provide a way out so that *you* can endure it." This verse says that God will always provide a way of escape for people, so that people cannot say that they *had* to do something wrong.

In Galatians 5:16-23, we are told that in order to avoid sexual sin, a man needs to yield to the influence of the Holy Spirit at work in his heart: "So I say, walk by the Spirit, and you will not gratify the desires of the flesh. For the flesh desires what is contrary to the Spirit... But the fruit of the Spirit is love, joy, peace, patience, kindness, goodness, faithfulness, gentleness and *self-control.*"

Jesus used the following *metaphor* to tell people that *they are each responsible to deal with their **own** issues*: "If *your* right eye causes you to lust, gouge it out and throw it away... And if *your* right hand causes you to sin, cut it off and throw it away. It is better for you to lose one part of your body than for your whole body to be thrown into hell" (Matthew 5:29-30). Jesus did *not* say to point the finger of blame towards others. In the New Testament, Jesus used this metaphor on two occasions--once when He was speaking to men about committing adultery (Matthew 5:27-30), and again when He was warning against child abuse (Mark 9:36-50; Matthew 18:1-14). It is better for people to face justice, taking responsibility for their own choices and behavior here on earth, than to deny their responsibility and later face God's vengeance on judgment day.

Freedom from Codependence

The destructive pattern of codependence is evident in so many areas. Wives are told they are responsible for their husband's violence and/or sexual problems. Husbands are told they are responsible for their wives' spiritual growth. Spiritual leaders feel they are responsible for their congregation members' choices. *We must realize that we cannot fix other people or be responsible for another adult's choices or behaviors.* Ministers can provide support, and share information and resources with an abused woman, who can then make her *own* choices. Her choices are between herself and God.

When we feel we are responsible for others' choices and behaviors, we can become controlling. People can also then blame us for their problems and behaviors, and they are unlikely to learn to take responsibility for themselves. Women *can* be responsible for their own spiritual growth. Men *are* responsible for their own criminal offenses, their own aggression, their own choices and their own sexual behaviors. *They* are responsible to seek help for their *own* issues.

To move out of the rescuer triangle, it can be helpful to ask ourselves, "What do *I* need to do to take care of *myself?*" People do need each other, and can ask each other for help when necessary, but *we are each*

47

responsible for ourselves and for getting the things we need, through respectful communication, boundary-setting and problem-solving.[79] **Interdependence is healthy, codependence is not**.

Some people feel lost and do not know what their role in life is if they are not "rescuing" or "leading" others. The Bible says our role in life is to know God's love for us, and love God in return, and to also love others equally to ourselves. We are to be led by the Holy Spirit--not by guilt, shame, a need for power, or a sense of obligation to others. Women may find the following self-talk helpful in trying to exit the "rescuer" role:

"I reject the role of being a rescuer. God says my role in life is to love Him, and then love others equally to myself. My needs and feelings are *equal* in importance to others' needs and feelings. I am *as* important as other people."

Also, "I reject the role of sex object. I am not an object or a slave. I belong to God as His beloved child, and I am honored by Him. As a woman I was *not* created for the purpose of serving and satisfying men. God created Adam and Eve to *share dominion* over the earth and to *rule together* (Genesis 1:26-28). Men and women were *both* created to love God and to love one another *equally*."

This kind of self-talk can help women to develop healthy internal boundaries, which can then help them to have healthy external boundaries.

7 Why Men Abuse

According to Anna Motz, author of "Toxic Couples: the Psychology of Domestic Violence," intimate partner violence stems from a number of possible factors: patriarchy, exposure to violence, trauma, and shame.[80] Patriarchy normalizes a power imbalance between men and women. Exposure to violence provides negative role-modeling. Violence and related trauma often result in internalized shame messages.

Shame is a lie about our identity. Some examples of shame messages include: "I am a failure, I am unlovable, I am worthless, etc." Children internalize shame messages by making sense of negative childhood experiences "egocentrically." In other words, they tend to think that bad experiences mean they themselves are bad or unacceptable. Shame messages are common, since no one has had a perfect childhood.

People who have internalized shame messages often punish themselves in various ways. In order to overcome shame, it can be helpful for people to identify their *own* internalized shame lies, understand where they originated, and work on challenging these lies with truth about their value in God's eyes.

It appears that many abusive men subconsciously *project* their shame onto their partners ("*you are* a failure, *you are* unlovable"), and then punish the object of their shame. People who place their own shame onto others do not take responsibility for their own problem with shame, and will not change because they only blame, control and punish the other person.

Psychotherapist Jim O'Shea explains,

> Abusive personality types have a dangerous and specific characteristic--the blaming mindset. *They project their own negative traits onto their partners.* This mindset sees the partner as the source of the abuser's discomfort, shortcomings and failures, and this continually stokes his anger...

> The abusive or controlling personality type believes the partner is the problem and must be controlled and made subject to his will.[81]

Partners, family members, friends and spiritual leaders cannot "fix" these people, who refuse to take full responsibility for their own words and actions, and who refuse to seek help for what is behind *their* abusive behavior.

Proverbs 29:22 says, "An angry man stirs up arguments, and a hot-tempered man *causes* many transgressions."

Proverbs 19:19 says, "A person with great anger bears the penalty; *if you rescue him*, you'll have to do it again."

The only hope for people who abuse is that they *stop blaming others* for their behavior, and that they *take full responsibility* for all of their words and actions. It is also important that they *seek help* to uncover and overcome their own shame messages and false beliefs. *No one can do this work for them.* The abuse is enabled when people blame the victim, or try to appease or "fix" the abuser.

8 Divorce

"God hates divorce." These three words, taken from a much larger passage in Malachi chapter 2, are sometimes used to tell women that they must remain in abusive relationships.

What is God actually saying in the book of Malachi?

> You cover the altar of the LORD with tears as you weep and groan, because He no longer pays any attention to the offering nor accepts it favorably from you. Yet you ask, "Why?" The LORD is testifying against you on behalf of the wife you married when you were young, to whom you have become unfaithful even though she is your companion and wife by law. No one who has even a small portion of the Spirit in him does this. What did our ancestor do when seeking a child from God? Be attentive, then, to your own spirit, for one should not be disloyal to the wife he took in his youth. "I hate divorce," says the LORD God of Israel, "and the one who is guilty of violence," says the LORD who rules over all. "Pay attention to your conscience, and do not be unfaithful." (Malachi 2:13-16)

God is actually rebuking men who are unfaithful and violent towards their wives.

Earlier in the passage, God compares this marital infidelity to Israel's sin of idolatry:

> Judah has become disloyal, and unspeakable sins have been committed in Israel and Jerusalem. For Judah has profaned the holy things that the LORD loves and has turned to a foreign god! May the LORD cut off from the community of Jacob every last person who does this, as well as the person who presents improper offerings to the LORD who rules over all! (Malachi 2:11-12)

In chapters 3 and 19 of the book of Jeremiah, God similarly rebukes Israel and Judah for worshiping idols (unfaithfulness), and offering their children as ritual sacrifices to false gods (violence). What was God's response to this behavior? "I gave wayward Israel her divorce papers and sent her away" (Jeremiah 3:8).[82]

God divorced those among His people who were guilty of infidelity and violence. Now, various church leaders are misquoting God to tell women to "submit to abuse."

Women are also often told that the Bible says believers can only divorce if their partner has an affair, or abandons them. People point to both

Matthew 5:31 and 1 Corinthians 7:15 to make this argument.

It is important to *be aware of what Jesus was addressing* in Matthew 5:31 to properly make sense of what was being said. The Jewish rabbis of the school of Hillel were teaching that as long as a man gave his wife a "get," or a writ of divorce, he could leave her *for any reason.* On the other hand, the Jewish school of Shammai taught that a man could divorce his wife only in the case of infidelity. (Women, in both rabbinic traditions, were not permitted to divorce their husbands by issuing a "get.")[83]

Jesus confronted the teaching of Hillel here, saying that men could not excuse themselves of their vows to their wives. *They may especially not do this simply because they wished to marry another woman.*

Jesus was saying that if a "get" was issued by the man, but not for legitimate reasons, then the couple was still legally married, and sexual relations with other parties would still be considered adultery.

His point was to **protect women** against the infidelity of their husbands, who attempted to excuse this by simply issuing a "get."

Similarly in Malachi 2:16, God was **protecting women** against a husband's infidelity and/or violence.

Neither of these passages can be properly used to tell women to stay in a relationship in which a man has violated the marriage covenant through infidelity or violence.

In 1 Corinthians 7:15, Paul was addressing Christians who were married to unbelievers. It is important to be aware of this context in order to understand how this passage can be properly applied to people's lives. The question Paul was addressing was not related to abuse; it concerned whether or not believers should stay with non-believing spouses. Paul told believers to stay with non-believing spouses, not to leave them. He then said, "but if the husband or wife who isn't a believer insists on leaving, let them go. In such cases the Christian husband or wife is no longer bound to the other, for God has called you to live in peace" (1 Corinthians 7:15). Christians abandoned by an unbelieving partner, were no longer "bound" to the marriage. They would be free to remarry if they chose.

Throughout 1st Corinthians chapter 7, Paul is addressing believers in Christ who wondered whether or not their new faith required them to be single and celibate. Paul said, "no." He encouraged people who were married to remain married. For those who were single but wished to marry, he said that this was also acceptable.

In all of the Bible passages reviewed concerning divorce, God *never* tells women that they are obligated to remain in an abusive relationship.

9 Identifying and Responding to Abuse

It is important for church leaders to be able to recognize abuse, and to learn how to respond in a helpful manner.

The following information is taken from an online article by Smith and Segal (2016) entitled, "Domestic Violence and Abuse":

General warning signs of domestic abuse

People who are being abused may:

- Seem afraid or anxious to please their partner
- Go along with everything their partner says and does
- Check in often with their partner to report where they are and what they're doing
- Receive frequent, harassing phone calls from their partner
- Talk about their partner's temper, jealousy, or possessiveness

Warning signs of physical violence

People who are being physically abused may:

- Have frequent injuries, with the excuse of "accidents"
- Frequently miss work, school, or social occasions, without explanation
- Dress in clothing designed to hide bruises or scars (e.g. wearing long sleeves in the summer or sunglasses indoors)

Warning signs of isolation

People who are being isolated by their abuser may:

- Be restricted from seeing family and friends
- Rarely go out in public without their partner
- Have limited access to money, credit cards, or the car

The psychological warning signs of abuse

People who are being abused may:

- Have very low self-esteem, even if they were formerly confident
- Show major personality changes (e.g. an outgoing person becomes withdrawn)
- Be depressed, anxious, or suicidal

If you suspect that someone you know is being abused, speak up. If you are hesitating--thinking that it is none of your business, that you might be wrong, or that the person might not want to talk about it-- keep in mind that expressing your concern will let the person know that you care and may even save her life. Remember, abusers are very good at controlling and manipulating their victims. People who have been abused may be depressed, drained, afraid, ashamed and/or confused. They may need help, but they may be isolated from their family and friends. By offering support, you can help them become aware of options that may promote their safety and healing.[84]

What to do if Someone is Being Abused

The Canadian Women's Foundation recommends the following response if you believe that a woman is experiencing domestic abuse:

- If someone is in immediate danger, you can call 911 or the emergency number in your community.

- Learn about emergency services in your community, such as your local women's shelter or sexual assault centre. Search online or consult the front pages of your telephone directory.

- Put safety first. Talk to the person in private. Never talk to anyone about abuse in front of a suspected abuser. Never give her information through voice messages or emails that might be discovered by her abuser. However, abuse thrives in secrecy, so speak up *if you can do so safely*. It may be helpful to say something like, "I am concerned that you are in abusive relationship. Is there anything I can do?"[85]

- If she wants to talk, listen. Tell her the violence is not her fault, and that she deserves to be treated with respect, no matter what. Let her know you do not blame her. Don't expect to know all the answers. Explore options with her. Don't try to take over or tell her what to do. Ask direct, simple questions such as: "Do you want me to help you find someone to talk to?" or "Do you want to go somewhere safe?"[86] If she isn't sure what to do, simply encourage her to talk, and listen without judgment. If she is open to support, you can share available resources (e.g. crisis lines, women's shelters, sexual assault support centers, etc.). (For information about crisis lines and women's shelters, see Appendix A.)

- If she does not want to talk, simply tell her she does not deserve to be harmed and that you are concerned for her safety. It may be helpful to say something like, "If you want to talk another time, I'm here and am ready to listen."[87] Ask her if there is anything you can do to help, but do not offer to do anything that makes you uncomfortable or feels unsafe.

- If she decides to stay in the relationship, do not judge her. Leaving an abuser can be very difficult and at times extremely dangerous. Sometimes, the most valuable thing you can offer a woman who is being abused is your respect.[88] (A woman may stay in an abusive relationship for a number of reasons. Many of these are mentioned in an article written by

Sandra Hawken for the Canadian Women's Foundation; see Appendix B.)

For Women who May be in an Abusive Relationship

The Canadian Women's Foundation explains,

> Abuse takes many forms. The harm you experience may be physical, sexual, emotional, financial or spiritual. Sometimes the abuse follows a pattern, sometimes it doesn't. The abuse may happen every day or occasionally. It doesn't matter--abuse is always wrong.
>
> Strange as it sounds, sometimes it's hard to recognize you are being abused. Many abusers say things like, "You are useless," or "You made me do this," or "It's your own fault," or "You deserve it." All of these statements…destroy your self-confidence and blame you for the abuse. The experience of being abused causes emotional harm that makes it difficult to see what's really going on.[89]

Smith and Segal provide the following questions to help you identify if you are experiencing abuse:

Your Inner Thoughts and Feelings

Do you:

- feel afraid of your partner much of the time?

- avoid certain topics out of fear of angering your partner?
- feel that you cannot do anything right for your partner?
- believe that you deserve to be hurt or mistreated?
- feel emotionally numb or helpless?

Belittling Behavior

Does your partner:

- humiliate or yell at you?
- criticize you and put you down?
- treat you so badly that you are embarrassed in front of your friends and family?
- ignore or put down your opinions or accomplishments?
- blame you for his own abusive behavior?
- treat you as property or a sex object, rather than as a person?

Violent Behavior or Threats

Does your partner:

- have a bad and unpredictable temper?
- hurt you, or threaten to hurt or kill you?

- threaten to take your children away or harm them?

- threaten to commit suicide if you leave?

- force you to have sex?

- destroy your belongings?

Controlling Behavior

Does your partner:

- act excessively jealous and possessive?

- control where you go or what you do?

- keep you from seeing your friends or family?

- limit your access to money, the phone, or the car?

- constantly check up on you?

The more you answer "yes" to these questions, the more likely it is that you are in an abusive relationship.[90] (To see what *Healthy Relationships* should look like, see Appendix C.)

The Cycle of Violence

It is important to recognize that domestic abuse can take place in a cyclical pattern that includes the following recurring stages (adapted from "The Cycle of Abuse," as shared at hiddenhurt.co.uk):

1) Tension Building

- Tension starts and steadily builds
- Abuser starts to get angry
- Communication breaks down
- Victim feels the need to concede to the abuser
- Victim feels uneasy and a need to watch every move

2) Incident or "Acting Out" Phase

- Any type of abuse occurs:
  - Physical
  - Sexual
  - Emotional
  - Spiritual

3) Honeymoon or Reconciliation Phase

- Abuser apologizes for abuse, may beg forgiveness
- Abuser may promise it will never happen again
- Abuser blames victim for provoking the abuse
- Abuser denies the abuse, or claims it was not as bad as the victim remembers

4) Calm Before the Tension Starts Again

- Abuse temporarily slows or stops
- Abuser acts like the abuse never happened

- Promises made during honeymoon stage may be met, for a time
- Abuser may give gifts to victim
- Victim believes or wants to believe the abuse is over or the abuser will change[91]

If There is Abuse, What Can You Do?

The following information is taken directly from The Canadian Women's Foundation's Tip Sheet: "Support for Abused Women":

Stay or Go?

There are many reasons why women stay in an abusive relationship. Maybe you've stayed because you are financially dependent on the abuser and cannot afford to leave. Maybe you love the abuser and don't want to leave the relationship--you just want the violence to stop. Perhaps you blame yourself. You may be physically dependent on the abuser. Maybe your abuser has threatened to kill you if you leave. Every woman has her own reasons, and every woman has the right to make her own decisions. But no matter how hopeless or trapped or frightened you feel, help is available.

Tell Someone

You can tell someone you trust about the abuse. This might be a friend, family member, teacher, nurse, doctor, or someone from your faith community. Before speaking to them, decide what you want them to do. Do you just want them to listen? Do you want help finding a lawyer or a new place to live? Think about what you want, then ask for it. If they try to pressure you into doing something that makes you uncomfortable or afraid, speak up. Tell them how this makes you feel. Ask them to respect your wishes. Only you can decide if and when you should leave. If they downplay the abuse, don't believe you, or refuse to help, tell someone else.

Discover Your Options

Before taking action, you can call a crisis line or women's shelter to find out your options. They will help you create a safety plan and learn about your rights. Abusers often lie to control their victims, so you cannot rely on what they say. For example, abusers often threaten to take custody of children or have someone deported when they actually have no such power. Make a list of your questions, then talk to an expert.

Protect Yourself

If you decide to leave the abuser, **create a safety plan**. Abusers often become more violent if they believe their victims are planning to leave. Take precautions to ensure they do not learn about your plans through voice messages, emails, texts, or your internet use. Your safety plan should include strategies for staying safe at every stage: while you are still in the relationship; as you prepare to leave; your actual departure; and afterwards. To learn more about safety planning, talk to a shelter or visit neighboursfriendsandfamily.ca. [92]

What a Safety Plan Might Look Like

Are you experiencing abuse by your partner, but aren't sure how to protect yourself or how to leave?

The following guidelines, developed by "Neighbours, Friends and Families," describe the actions you can take to protect your safety and the safety of your children; they also describe how you can develop a plan to leave the abusive relationship:

Developing a Safety Plan

Safety planning is a top priority, whether you choose to remain in the home or leave. Making a safety plan involves identifying actions to increase your safety and that of your children.

Below are some suggestions that might be helpful to you. Take one action at a time and start with the one that is easiest and safest for you.

Protecting yourself while living with an abuser:

- Tell someone you trust about the abuse.
- Think about your partner's past use and level of force. This will help you predict what type of danger you and your children are facing and when to leave.

- Tell your children that abuse is never right, even when someone they love is being abusive. Tell them the abuse isn't your fault or their fault; they did not cause it, and neither did you. Teach them it is important to keep safe when there is abuse.

- Plan where to go in an emergency. Teach your children how to get help. Tell them not to get between you and your partner if there is violence. Plan a code word to signal they should get help or leave.

- Don't run to a place where the children are, as your partner may hurt them as well.

- Create a plan to get out of your home safely and practice it with your children.

- Ask your neighbours, friends and family to call the police if they hear sounds of abuse and to look after your children in an emergency.

- If an argument is developing, move to a space where you can get outside easily.

- Don't go to a room where there is access to potential weapons (e.g. kitchen, workshop, bathroom).

- If you are being hurt, protect your face with your arms around each side of your head, with your fingers locked together. Don't wear scarves or long jewelry.

- Park your car by backing it into the driveway and keep it fuelled.

- Hide your keys, cell phone and some money near your escape route.

- Have a list of phone numbers to call for help. Call the police if it is an emergency.

- Your local shelter or police may be able to equip you with a panic button/cell phone.

- Make sure all weapons and ammunition are hidden or removed from your home.

Getting Ready to Leave

When you are planning to leave, here are some suggestions:

- Contact the police or a local women's shelter. Let the staff know that you intend to leave an abusive situation and ask for support in safety planning. Ask for an officer who specializes in woman abuse cases (information shared with the police may result in charges being laid against the abuser).

- If you are injured, go to a doctor or an emergency room and report what happened to you. Ask them to document your visit.

- Gather important documents:
  - identification, bank cards, financial papers related to family assets, last...Income Tax Return, keys, medication, pictures of the abuser and your children, passports, health cards, personal address/telephone book, cell

phone, and legal documents (e.g. immigration papers, house deed/lease, restraining orders/peace bonds).

- If you can't keep these things stored in your home for fear your partner will find them, consider making copies and leave them with someone you trust. Your local women's shelter will also keep them for you.

- Consult a lawyer. Keep any evidence of physical abuse (such as photos). Keep a journal of all violent incidents, noting dates, events, threats and any witnesses.

- Put together pictures, jewelry and objects of sentimental value, as well as toys and comforts for your children.

- Arrange with someone to care for your pets temporarily, until you get settled. A shelter may help with this.

- Remember to clear your phone of the last number you called to avoid his utilizing redial.

Leaving the Abuser

Here are some suggestions for your personal safety when you leave:

- Request a police escort or ask a friend, neighbour or family member to accompany you when you leave.

- Contact your local women's shelter. It may be a safer temporary spot than going to a place your partner knows.

- Do not tell your partner you are leaving.

- Leave quickly.

- Have a back-up plan if your partner finds out where you are going.

After Leaving

Here are some actions you should take after you or your partner has left the relationship:

- Visit the closest police station and ask to speak to an officer who specializes in woman abuse cases.

- Consider applying for a restraining order or peace bond that may help keep your partner away from you and your children. Keep it with you at all times.

- Provide police with a copy of any legal orders you have.

- Consult a lawyer or legal aid clinic about actions to protect yourself or your children. Let your lawyer know if there are any Criminal Court proceedings.

- Consider changing any service provider that you share with your ex-partner.

- Obtain an unlisted telephone number, get caller ID and block your number when calling out.

- Make sure your children's school or day care centre is aware of the situation and has copies of all relevant documents.

- Carry a photo of the abuser and your children with you.

- Ask your neighbours to look after your children in an emergency and to call the police if they see the abuser.

- Take extra precautions at work, at home and in the community. Consider telling your supervisor at work about your situation.

- Think about places and patterns that your ex-partner will know about and try to change them. For example, consider using a different grocery store or place of worship.

- If you feel unsafe walking alone, ask a neighbour, friend or family member to accompany you.

- Do not return to your home unless accompanied by the police. Never confront the abuser. [93]

10 The Danger of Enabling Abuse

It is of utmost importance for church leaders to recognize abuse, and to provide well-informed support for abuse victims. There has been a sad tendency in the church to deny or minimize abuse, and defend the offender. Referring to the ABC News investigation on domestic violence and the church, Joanna Cruickshank (Senior Lecturer at Deakin University) explains,

> Multiple women have courageously told their stories of experiencing violence from men quoting Scripture--and of clergy and other Christians who have enabled this abuse to continue. I honour these women, many of whom understandably fear for their lives and that of their children, but who have shared their story in the hope of bringing about change. Their accounts point not only to perpetrators within the church, but to a culture in which their cries for help have sometimes been met with scepticism or denial, with platitudes about forgiveness and with accusations that they are doing harm to the church.[94]

Proverbs 28:16 says, "A leader who lacks understanding is very oppressive." Proverbs 19:19

warns against protecting angry men from the consequences of their actions: "A man of great wrath will suffer punishment; for if you deliver him you will have to do it again." Christian leaders who are uninformed about the dynamics of domestic violence run the risk of enabling the abuse to continue. All church leaders *must* become educated in the area of domestic violence.

11 Conclusion

The book of Genesis shows us that as a result of sin entering the world, men would try to dominate women, and abusers would seek to shift the blame and justify their wrong behavior.[95] Jesus regularly spoke out against oppressive power, and said that He came to set the captives free (Luke 4:18-21). Spiritually speaking, Jesus broke down the walls between Jews and Gentiles, between slaves and free, and between men and women (Ephesians 2:14; Galatians 3:28). There is not to be any power imbalance between husbands and wives. Adam and Eve were created to *rule together*, and to *share dominion* over the earth (Genesis 1:26-28). Paul says marriage is to be "an illustration of the way Christ and the church are one" (Ephesians 5:32). Husbands are to love and serve their wives, as Jesus loved and served the church. Wives are then to also love and serve their husbands. It is a picture of *mutual* love and service.

Women in some churches today are given false information about "submission," "headship," and "marital permanence." Abusive men take advantage of these harmful *mistranslations* and *misinterpretations* of the Bible to justify their violent and controlling behavior towards their wives. It is important for spiritual leaders to correct these misinterpretations, and to teach that "coercive control and violence are *never* acceptable."[96] Spiritual leaders must also become educated about domestic violence, and be armed with training and resources to deal with this issue, which is very close to the heart of God. Church leaders should not ignore "the fact that these matters are criminal behaviors; and that they have very real long-term consequences for the victims."[97]

In Ezekiel 34:1-22, God addresses shepherds who have failed to protect the sheep--the vulnerable members of their community. God says, "You have not taken care of the weak. You have not tended the sick or bound up the injured... You abandoned my flock and left them to be attacked... So I will rescue my flock, and they will no longer be abused." Jesus said how we treat others is also how we treat Him, and that we will be held accountable for what we say and do to others (Matthew 25:40). Society already tends to blame the victim: "What did you do to cause this violence?" God does *not* blame the victim; the church must follow God's example. Spiritual leaders must stand up for the oppressed and hold abusers accountable for their *own* actions, as God does.

Highlighting the need for greater awareness about domestic violence in the church is *not* an attack on Christianity. Rather, it acknowledges that the Christian faith has been *misrepresented*, and the Bible *misused* to justify and enable abuse. "God help us as Christians if we cannot acknowledge our failures."[98]

Women need to be given *accurate* information, so that they can make *informed* decisions: "Those who are prudent see danger and take refuge" (Proverbs 27:12). Jesus came to *set the oppressed free*. The *safety* of domestic abuse victims *must* be the church's priority.

Barbara Roberts, domestic violence prevention advocate, highlights the need for greater discernment on the part of church leaders:

> Jesus told his followers they needed to be wise as serpents and harmless as doves, but most churches are not wise about the mentality and tactics of evildoers, nor are they aware of how evildoers masquerade as believers in the church. The abuser typically has a Dr Jekyll persona that depicts him (or occasionally her) as a wonderful and godly man, so that no-one would suspect the truth... If the victim reports the abuse to church leaders, the abuser is skilled at shifting blame, evading accountability, and pretending repentance and reformation. The vast majority of church leaders aren't discerning enough to detect these tactics of abusers for what they are: lies, [and] often advise the victim to remain with or return to the abuser.[99]

God addresses those who use religion as a cover for abuse in Isaiah 29:13-21:

> These people say they are mine. They honor me with their lips, but their hearts are far from

> Me. Their worship is a farce, for they teach
> man-made ideas as commands from God...
> Soon, and it will not be long... The scoffer
> will be gone, the arrogant will disappear, and
> those who plot evil will be killed. Those who
> convict the innocent by their false testimony
> will disappear. A similar fate awaits those
> who use trickery to pervert justice and who
> tell lies to destroy the innocent.

God promises that one day, He will take vengeance against those who are abusive, are not remorseful, and are not willing to change their behavior (Romans 12:19).

God also rebukes spiritual leaders who worship Him while allowing injustice and unrighteousness to continue. In Amos 5:21-24 God says,

> I hate all your show and pretense--the
> hypocrisy of your religious festivals and
> solemn assemblies...
> Away with your noisy hymns of praise!
> I will not listen to the music of your harps.
> Instead, I want to see a mighty flood of
> justice, an endless river of righteous living.

It is important that church leaders not avoid the topic of domestic violence, but take a leadership role in educating their congregations about abuse, and the importance of equal, loving and respectful relationships.

A victim's faith and the support of her church community can be vital to her healing process. Shelters and other domestic violence services can also be vital in providing safety, information and support. It is our prayer that churches and domestic violence services will work together, so that abused women of faith can find both freedom and hope.

Appendix A

The following definitions are taken directly from the Canadian Women's Foundation at canadianwomen.org:

Crisis Lines: Many communities (and some women's shelters) have a 24-hour telephone crisis line. These services are confidential--you don't need to give your name or phone number. They will listen, answer your questions, and refer you to the services you're looking for. Look in the front of your phone book, or search online for crisis lines in your community.

Women's Shelters/Transition Houses: A women's shelter, sometimes called a transition house, is a special, secure residence designed especially for women who are escaping abusive relationships. They offer women and their children a safe place to sleep, food, clothes, and basic supplies. They also provide counseling, safety planning, and can help women to find housing, employment training, legal support, advice on immigration issues, and other community resources. Look in the front of your phone book, or search online for women's shelters or transition houses in your community. If you are in an area that has no shelter or transition house, find out about other agencies offering specialized services for victims of abuse in the phone book, or search online.[100]

Appendix B

Writing for the Canadian Women's Foundation online blog, Sandra Hawken explains why women have difficulty leaving an abusive relationship:

Too many people assume that if a woman is in an abusive relationship, [then] she is making a choice to stay and that she has the power to end the abuse if she just leaves.

Canadian Women's Foundation studies shows 67 per cent of us know a woman who has been abused. Domestic violence is an epidemic...because it is rarely as easy as "just leaving."

So why doesn't she just leave?

- She may stay because she fears for her life or the life of her children, because he's threatened what he might do if she dares try to leave.

- She may stay because she believes she has nowhere to go. She might not know how the community can support her, or the local shelter might be full.

- She may stay because everyone thinks her abuser is a "good guy," and she feels ashamed and embarrassed and is sure she'll be judged and not believed if she speaks out about the abuse.

- She may stay because she's willing to sacrifice her own safety for the well being of her children so they won't have to grow up in poverty or without a father.

- She may stay because her family, friends or community have told her they won't support her and that they believe divorce is never a viable option.

- She may stay because of her immigration status or because her first language isn't English to be able to reach out for help.

- She may stay because she has a disability and is dependent on him for daily care.

- She may stay because she grew up in a family where abuse was normal, making it hard to recognize when a relationship is unhealthy.

- She may stay because she loves him and he seems to regret the violence. She may want to try to make the relationship work and help him to change.

- She may stay because she blames herself. She's been told it's her fault and that she deserves to be abused.

It's time to stop the victim-blaming.

We *should* be asking, "Why is he abusive?" or "How can we break the cycle of violence?" or "How can I support her to be safe?"

We also need to ask ourselves why these questions seem so scary. I believe it's because they--finally-- upset the status quo, and shine the light on the real problem.[101]

Appendix C

The Canadian Women's Foundation shares the
following guidelines to help identify what healthy
relationships looks like:

Healthy Relationships Are:

HONEST
We share how we feel.
We tell the truth.
We take responsibility for our actions.

SAFE
We respect each other's boundaries (physical,
emotional, sexual).
We control our anger.
We never use intimidation, threats, or violence.

RESPECTFUL
We value each other's feelings.
We value each other's opinion.
We admit when we are wrong.

FAIR
We compromise.
We share decision-making.
We each do our part.

SUPPORTIVE
We listen without judging.
We believe in one another.
We care if the other is happy.[102]

ABOUT THE AUTHORS

Helga and Bob Edwards have been married since 1988. They have been Therapists and Public Speakers since 1996. Both have Bachelor's degrees in Religious Education and Social Development Studies, as well as Master's degrees in Social Work. In 2013, they each received the Delta Epsilon Chi Award for Intellectual Achievement, Christian Character and Leadership Ability, from the Association for Biblical Higher Education. Their hope is to use the gifts and training that God has given them to help people experience freedom and wholeness in their lives. Feel free to visit their website at www.awakedeborah.com.

Helga and Bob have also written "The Equality Workbook: Freedom in Christ from the Oppression of Patriarchy." The workbook was written to help readers identify and remove patriarchal bias from Bible translation and commentary. Bible passages that have been overlooked, misinterpreted or altered in translation to make patriarchy (the rule of men) appear to be "the will of God" include the following:

Genesis chapters 1, 2, 3, 21 and 24
Judges chapters 2, 4, 5, 19 and 20
Isaiah chapter 3
Joel chapter 2
Ezekiel chapter 34
Zechariah chapter 5
Matthew chapters 10, 20, 23 and 28
Luke chapters 13 and 24
John chapter 13
Acts chapters 1, 2, 11, 18, 19 and 28
Romans chapters 1 and 16

1 Corinthians chapters 1, 3, 7, 10, 11 and 14
2 Corinthians chapter 3
Ephesians chapters 3 and 5
Colossians chapter 3
Philippians chapters 1, 2 and 4
1 Timothy chapters 1, 2, 3, 4, 5 and 6
2 Timothy chapter 2
Titus chapter 2
Galatians chapters 2, 3 and 5
1 Peter chapters 2 and 3

As patriarchal bias is removed, it will become evident that far from being the will of God, "the rule of men" is a human tradition rooted in prejudice.

The workbook also focuses on helping women recover from the harmful effects of patriarchy. To help with the recovery process, the following topics are explored:

• overcoming the lies of shame
• suffering
• the grief process
• rejecting patriarchal stereotypes
• managing triggers
• setting boundaries
• freedom from codependence
• healthy egalitarian relationships
• communication and problem-solving
• overcoming negative patterns in relationships
• living in balance.

Women are encouraged to be empowered by God to bring healing and freedom to the world in Jesus' name.

[1] Nash, S., Faulkner, C. & Abell, R. "Abused Conservative Christian Wives: Treatment Considerations for Practitioners." Counseling and Values, Volume 58, October 2013, American Counseling Association.

[2] Stetzer, E. "The Church and its Response to Domestic and Sexual Violence: Pastors must address domestic and sexual violence." Christianity Today, June 20, 2014, http://www.christianitytoday.com/edstetzer/2014/june/church-and-its-response-to-domestic-and-sexual-violence.html.

[3] United Nations, General Assembly: Declaration on the Elimination of Violence against Women, December 20th, 1993, http://www.un.org/documents/ga/res/48/a48r104.htm.

[4] Baird J. & Gleeson, H. "'Submit to your husbands': Women told to endure domestic violence in the name of God." ABC News: 7.30, Updated 10 Aug 2017, http://www.abc.net.au/news/2017-07-18/domestic-violence-church-submit-to-husbands/8652028.

[5] Canadian Women's Foundation: The Facts About Violence Against Women, http://www.canadianwomen.org/facts-about-violence.

[6] Family Violence in Canada, A Statistical Profile, 2013. Available at: http://www.statcan.gc.ca/pub/85-002-x/2014001/article/14114-eng.pdf

[7] Measuring Violence Against Women: Statistical Trends, 2013, Statistics Canada, p.8. http://www.statcan.gc.ca/pub/85-002-x/2013001/article/11766-eng.pdf

[8] "Police-reported dating violence in Canada, 2008," Tina Hotton Mahony, Juristat, Canadian Centre for Justice Statistics, Volume 30 Number 2, page 7. Available: http://www.statcan.gc.ca/pub/85-002-x/2010002/article/11242-eng.pdf.

[9] Family Violence in Canada, A Statistical Profile, 2013, Statistics Canada. Available at: http://www.statcan.gc.ca/pub/85-002-x/2014001/article/14114-eng.pdf.

[10] Anxiety and Depression Association of America: Symptoms of PTSD, April 2016, https://adaa.org/understanding-anxiety/posttraumatic-stress-disorder-ptsd/symptoms

[11] World Health Organization: Global and Regional Estimates of Violence Against Women, 2013, http://apps.who.int/iris/bitstream/10665/85239/1/9789241564625_eng.pdf.

[12] Canadian Women's Foundation: The Facts About Violence Against Women, http://www.canadianwomen.org/facts-about-violence.

[13] Measuring Violence Against Women: Statistical Trends 2013, p. 86. Available: http://www.statcan.gc.ca/pub/85-002-x/2013001/article/11766-eng.pdf.

[14] The Association Between Adverse Childhood Experiences (ACEs) and Suicide Attempts in a Population-based Study, 2016, Child: Care, Health and Development, summary available at: https://www.sciencedaily.com/releases/2016/06/160609115306.htm?utm_source=feedburner&utm_mediu m=email&utm_campaign=Feed%3A+sciencedaily%2Fmind_brain%2Frelationships+%28Relationships+News+--+ScienceDaily%29.

[15] PTSD, Other Disorders Evident in Kids Who Witness Domestic Violence," Eve Bender, Psychiatric News, American Psychiatric Association, June 4, 2004, p. 14. Available: http://psychnews.psychiatryonline.org/doi/full/10.1176/pn.39.11.0390014a?trendmd-shared=1&.

[16] PTSD Symptoms in Young Children Exposed to Intimate Partner Violence, By Alytia A. Levendosky , G. Anne Bogat and Cecilia Martinez-Torteya2, 2013, p 1-2 Available at: https://www.researchgate.net/profile/G_Anne_Bogat/

publication/235659438_PTSD_Symptoms_in_Young
_Children_Exposed_to_Intimate_Partner_Violence/li
nks/55ba8a6b08ae092e965dac1f.pdf.

[17] The Effects of Family Violence on Children: Where
Does it Hurt, Royal Canadian Mounted Police, 2012,
Available at: http://www.rcmp-grc.gc.ca/cp-pc/chi-
enf-abu-eng.htm.

[18] Child Abuse/Children Exposed to Violence
Information Sheet, Human Services Alberta, October
2008 Available at:
http://www.humanservices.alberta.ca/documents/PFV
B0399-children-exposed-to-family-violence.pdf.

[19] Child Abuse/Children Exposed to Violence
Information Sheet, Human Services Alberta, October
2008 Available at:
http://www.humanservices.alberta.ca/documents/PFV
B0399-children-exposed-to-family-violence.pdf.

[20] Baird & Gleeson, 2017.

[21] Baird & Gleeson, 2017.

[22] Baird and Gleeson, 2017.

[23] Stetzer, 2014.

[24] Tracy, S. "Patriarchy and Domestic Violence:
Challenging Common Misconceptions." The Journal

of the Evangelical Theological Society 50/3, pp. 573-594, September, 2007.

[25] Edwards, H. and Edwards, B. (2016). The Equality Workbook: Freedom in Christ from the Oppression of Patriarchy. Charleston, SC: Createspace.

[26] Christianity Today. "Theodosias I, Emperor who Made Christianity 'the' Roman Religion," Christian History: http://www.christianitytoday.com/history/people/rulers/theodosius-i.html.

[27] Gardner, J. (1995). Women in Roman Law and Society. Indianapolis, Indiana: Indiana University Press.

[28] Sedley, D. (2016). Routledge Encyclopedia of Philosophy: Ancient Philosophy, https://www.rep.routledge.com/articles/ancient-philosophy/v-1.

[29] Plato, The Republic, The Electronic Classical Series, Jim Manus Editor, Hazelton, PA: Pennsylvania State University, p. 117.

[30] Plato, The Republic.

[31] Plato, The Republic, p. 170.

[32] Plato, The Republic, p. 130.

[33] Plotinus, 1st Ennead: The "Soul" must exercise "single lordship" over the "Animate." "The Soul is evil by being interfused with the body." "Likeness to God" is experienced when "the Soul" is made "immune to passion." 4th Ennead: "Woman" is associated with matter, and portrayed as a "fetter" that draws the Soul away from the "Intellectual Realm." "Woman" is "Pandora" who is accused of opening the ill-fated box and releasing all the evils in the world. For more on Pandora, see: http://www.theoi.com/Heroine/Pandora.html. Plotinus' Enneads are available here: http://classics.mit.edu/Plotinus/enneads.html.

[34] Plotinus, Fifth Ennead, http://classics.mit.edu/Plotinus/enneads.5.fifth.html.

[35] Schatkin, M. (1970). The Influence of Origen upon St. Jerome's Commentary on Galatians. Vigiliae Christianae 24: 49-58; Heine, R. (2002). The Commentaries of Origen and Jerome on St. Paul's Letter to the Ephesians. Oxford University Press; as cited in Levy, I. (2011). The Letter to the Galatians. Grand Rapids, MI: Wm. B. Eerdmans Publishing Co.

[36] https://www.britannica.com/biography/Origen.

[37] Internet Encyclopedia of Philosophy: Origen of Alexandria, http://www.iep.utm.edu/origen-of-alexandria/#H3.

[38] https://www.britannica.com/biography/Plotinus.

[39] Edwards, B. (2015). A God I'd Like to Meet: Separating the Love of God from Harmful Traditional Beliefs. Charlotte NC: Createspace.

[40] Augustine, Confessions, Book 7, Chapter XX.

[41] Tracy, p. 587.

[42] Calvin, Institutes of the Christian Religion, Book III: "Augustine alone will suffice."

[43] Eire, C. (1989). War Against the Idols. Cambridge, UK: Cambridge University Press, p. 32.

[44] Edwards, B. (2015).

[45] Edwards H. & Edwards, B. (2016).

[46] In his online article entitled "The Myth of Mutual Submission," Complementarian Wayne Grudem claims, "the Greek text clearly specifies a restriction, 'Wives, be subject to your own husbands,'" http://gospeltranslations.org/wiki/The_Myth_of_Mutual_Submission.

[47] "P46 is a papyrus manuscript which dates from about 200. It is one of the oldest manuscripts we have. B is Codex Vaticanus, which is one of the best manuscripts we have, dating from about the fourth

century. Neither of these manuscripts has a verb in verse 22," http://episcopalarchives.org/cgi-bin/the_living_church/TLCarticle.pl?volume=221&issue=15&article_id=10; Photograph of Parchment 46: http://earlybible.com/manuscripts/p46-Eph-10.html; Cambridge Bible for Schools and Colleges: "It is probable that the Gr. original has no verb here," http://biblehub.com/commentaries/ephesians/5-22.htm; Nestle GNT "Αἱ γυναῖκες τοῖς ἰδίοις ἀνδράσιν," http://biblehub.com/nestle/ephesians/5.htm.

[48] The first instance on record of a second command "submit" being inserted into the Greek text of Ephesians 5:22 occurs in the middle of the 4th century A.D.. This alteration of the Greek coincides with the shift in Bible translation and commentary that we find in the 4th century work of St. Augustine and St. Jerome.

[49] Hart, https://godswordtowomen.org/subject_to_their_own_husbands.pdf, pp. 3-4.

[50] http://biblehub.com/greek/3784.htm; http://biblehub.com/greek/1163.htm.

[51] New American Standard Bible: Text Edition with Illustrated Dictionary-Concordance (1977). New York, NY: The Lockman Foundation, Thomas Nelson Publishers, p. X & 819.

[52] Parallel Greek texts of Ephesians 5:24,
http://biblehub.com/texts/ephesians/5-24.htm.

[53] Aristotle, Politics, Book I, Part II, translated by
Benjamin Jowett,
http://classics.mit.edu/Aristotle/politics.1.one.html.

[54] Philo, Questions and Answers on Genesis,
http://www.earlyjewishwritings.com/text/philo/book4
1.html.

[55] http://biblehub.com/greek/4646.htm.

[56] Cline, G. "The Middle Voice in the New
Testament," Submitted in partial fulfillment of
requirements for the degree of Master of Theology in
Grace Theological Seminary, May 1983. Digitized by
Ted Hildebrandt, Gordon College, 2006.

[57] Liddell-Scott-Jones Definitions,
https://www.studylight.org/lexicons/greek/4240.html.

[58] Xenophon of Athens, Cyropaedia VIII, 18, Loeb
Classics,
https://www.loebclassics.com/view/xenophon_athens-
cyropaedia/1914/pb_LCL052.315.xml.

[59] Liddell-Scott-Jones Lexicon,
http://www.perseus.tufts.edu/hopper/morph?l=u%28p
akou%2Fein&la=greek&can=u%28pakou%2Fein0&
prior=toiou/tois&d=Perseus:text:1999.01.0203:book=

8:chapter=1:section=18&i=1#lexicon, and
http://www.perseus.tufts.edu/hopper/morph?l=a%29k
ou%2Fseien&la=greek&can=a%29kou%2Fseien0&p
rior=de\&d=Perseus:text:1999.01.0203:book=8:chapt
er=1:section=18&i=1#lexicon.

[60] Genesis 21:12, LXX,
https://www.ellopos.net/elpenor/physis/septuagint-
genesis/21.asp?pg=2.

[61] Custis James, C. (2015). Malestrom: Manhood
Swept into the Currents of a Changing World. Grand
Rapids, MI: Zondervan, p. 57.

[62] Plutarch. Plutarch's Lives. with an English
Translation by. Bernadotte Perrin. Cambridge, MA.
Harvard University Press. London. William
Heinemann Ltd. 1914. 1,
http://www.perseus.tufts.edu/hopper/text?doc=Plut.%
20Thes.%201&lang=original

[63] Archon as "ruler":
http://biblehub.com/greek/758.htm.

[64] Aristotle, On the Cosmos, LCL 401a.

[65] Herodotus, The Histories, 4.91.

[66] Karpman, S.
https://www.karpmandramatriangle.com/.

[67] Beattie, M. (1992). Co-Dependent No More. Centre City, Minnesota: Hazelden.

[68] Edwards H. & Edwards, B. (2016).

[69] Aeschines. Aeschines with an English translation by Charles Darwin Adams, Ph.D. Cambridge, MA, Harvard University Press; London, William Heinemann Ltd. 1919, http://www.perseus.tufts.edu/hopper/text?doc=Perseus%3Atext%3A1999.01.0002%3Aspeech%3D3%3Asection%3D130.

[70] Plato. Platonis Opera, ed. John Burnet. Oxford University Press. 1903, http://www.perseus.tufts.edu/hopper/text?doc=Perseus%3Atext%3A1999.01.0177%3Atext%3DGorg.%3Asection%3D461e.

[71] Demosthenes. Demosthenes with an English translation by A. T. Murray, Ph.D., LL.D. Cambridge, MA, Harvard University Press; London, William Heinemann Ltd. 1939, http://www.perseus.tufts.edu/hopper/text?doc=Perseus%3Atext%3A1999.01.0074%3Aspeech%3D23%3Asection%3D57.

[72] Aristotle. Aristotle's Eudemian Ethics, ed. F. Susemihl. Leipzig: Teubner. 1884, http://www.perseus.tufts.edu/hopper/text?doc=Perseus

s%3Atext%3A1999.01.0049%3Abook%3D1%3Asect
ion%3D1216a.

[73] Strabo. ed. A. Meineke, Geographica. Leipzig:
Teubner. 1877,
http://www.perseus.tufts.edu/hopper/text?doc=Perseu
s%3Atext%3A1999.01.0197%3Abook%3D1%3Acha
pter%3D2%3Asection%3D17.

[74] "'It is good for a man not to touch a woman' may
be a quotation taken by Paul directly from the
Corinthians' letter to him. That Paul radically
qualifies this statement in verses 2-5, while at the
same time shifting from its male-only perspective to a
mutual perspective including both men and women
seems to confirm this. All of this suggests the strong
possibility that the statement was a slogan or motto
(ESV, HCSB, MOFFATT, NAB, NET, NRSV, REB,
TNIV; Collings, 252-53; Fee, 275-76; Garland, 248-
51; Thiselton, 498-500; c.f. the slogan/rebuttal tactic
in 6:12, 13, 18) of an ascetic wing of the Corinthians
church who not only advocated that married couples
should abstain from sexual relations (as implied by
vv. 2-5) but who also suggested that marriage was sin
(c.f. vv. 28, 36, 39) and that existing marriage should
be dissolved (vv. 10-16, 39; Fee 268-71, 275-77;
Hays 113-16). Bock, D. ed., (2006) The Bible
Knowledge Word Study: Acts-Ephesians, Colorado
Springs, Colorado: Victor, p. 253.

[75] Baird & Gleeson, 2017.

[76] Kiffe, B. "Marital Rape." Minnesota Coalition Against Sexual Assault, http://www.wcsap.org/sites/default/files/uploads/working_with_survivors/intimate_partner_sexual_violence/MaritalRapeMinnesota.pdf.

[77] Kiffe, B.

[78] Kiffe B.

[79] Beattie, 1992.

[80] Motz, A. (2014). Toxic Couples, the Psychology of Domestic Violence. Hove, East Sussex: Routledge, p. 155.

[81] Jim O'Shea Counselling Service: "Controlling people have low self-esteem and project their own negative traits onto their partners," August 15, 2015.

[82] It is important to recognize that Malachi uses a metaphor here to describe "*wayward* Israel." This is a reference to those within the nation of Israel who had practiced infidelity and violence, turning away from God to the worship of idols. God is not "divorcing" the entire nation, or an entire people group. To believe this would be to overgeneralize from the metaphor. In Malachi chapter 3, God reveals that those who remain faithful to Him will not be sent away (given a writ of divorce). They would continue to be God's people, and His relationship with them

would be unbroken. A similar pattern is found in the
New Testament. Although many of the Jewish scribes
and Pharisees viewed Jesus as a threat to their power
and did not believe in Him; all of His initial
followers--like Jesus himself--were Jewish.
Throughout the Bible, those within Israel who remain
faithful to God continue to be referred to as God's
"special treasure" (Malachi 3:17).

[83] Hillel, V. Kesher: A Journal of Messianic Judaism,
A Messianic Jewish View of Divorce. Issue 29, 2015.
http://www.kesherjournal.com/index.php?option=com
_content&view=article&id=179&Itemid=456.

[84] Melinda Smith, M.A., and Jeanne Segal, Ph.D. Last
updated: October 2016. Adapted from: NYS Office
for the Prevention of Domestic Violence,
http://www.helpguide.org/articles/abuse/domestic-
violence-and-abuse.htm.

[85] Canadian Women's Foundation: How to Help
Someone Living with Violence,
http://www.canadianwomen.org/sites/canadianwomen
.org/files/CWF-Avon-TipSheet-EN-web.pdf

[86] Canadian Women's Foundation: How to Help
Someone Living with Violence,
http://www.canadianwomen.org/sites/canadianwomen
.org/files/CWF-Avon-TipSheet-EN-web.pdf

[87] Canadian Women's Foundation: How to Help Someone Living with Violence, http://www.canadianwomen.org/sites/canadianwomen.org/files/CWF-Avon-TipSheet-EN-web.pdf

[88] Canadian Women's Foundation: The Facts About Violence Against Women, http://www.canadianwomen.org/facts-about-violence?gclid=CNG0-P3f1c8CFQyRaQod7KoKpA.

[89] Canadian Women's Foundation: Support for Abused Women, http://www.canadianwomen.org/sites/canadianwomen.org/files/CWF-Avon-TipSheet2-EN-web-final.pdf.

[90] Smith and Segal, 2016.

[91] Hiddenhurt.org: The Cycle of Abuse, http://www.hiddenhurt.co.uk/cycle_of_abuse.html

[92] Canadian Women's Foundation: Support for Abused Women, http://www.canadianwomen.org/sites/canadianwomen.org/files/CWF-Avon-TipSheet2-EN-web-final.pdf.

[93] Neighbours, Friends and Family: Safety Planning, http://www.neighboursfriendsandfamilies.ca/about/list-nff-communities?q=how-to-help/safety-planning.

[94] Cruickshank, J. "How Churches Enable Domestic Violence." ABC News, Religion and Ethics: July 26,

2017,
http://www.abc.net.au/religion/articles/2017/07/26/47
07934.htm.

[95] Tracy, 2007.

[96] Baird & Gleeson, 2017.

[97] Retired Bishop John Harrower, in Baird and
Gleeson, 2017.

[98] Tracy, S. "Asking Christians to do better by
domestic violence victims is not an attack on
Christianity." ABC News: July 27, 2017,
http://www.abc.net.au/news/2017-07-28/not-an-
attack-on-christianity-to-call-out-domestic-
violence/8751856.

[99] Baird and Gleeson, 2017.

[100] Canadian Women's Foundation: How to Help
Someone Living with Violence,
http://www.canadianwomen.org/sites/canadianwomen
.org/files/CWF-Avon-TipSheet-EN-web.pdf.

[101] Sandra Hawken, "Why Women Stay in Abusive
Relationships," Canadian Women's Foundation blog,
November 26,2013,
        http://www.canadianwomen.org/blog/why-
women-stay-abusive-relationships.

[102] Canadian Women's Foundation: Healthy Relationships Are, http://canadianwomen.org/sites/canadianwomen.org/files//Healthy%20Relationships%20Are.pdf.

God says, "As a mother comforts her child, so I will comfort you" (Isaiah 66:13). "See, I will not forget you… I have carved you on the palm of My hand" (Isaiah 49:16).

"God will rejoice over you with gladness, He will quiet you with His love, He will rejoice over you with singing" (Zephaniah 3:17).

Made in the USA
Middletown, DE
09 January 2018